This Love Changes Everything

Jane L. Fryar

This is love, not that we have loved God but that he loved us.

1 John 4:10

Prayer Journal

CTA

The mission of CTA
is to glorify God by providing purposeful products
that lift up and encourage the body of Christ —
because we love him.

www.CTAinc.com

This
Love
Changes Everything
Jane L. Fryar

Prayer Journal

Copyright © 2015 CTA, Inc.
1625 Larkin Williams Rd.
Fenton, MO 63026

PRINTED IN THAILAND
ISBN: 978-1-94088-23-5

This *Love* Changes Everything

Our culture is often quick to dismiss traditions, especially religious traditions, as irrelevant or outdated. But just as clichés become clichés because their usefulness invites repetition after repetition after repetition, traditions become traditions because those who practice them find increasing meaning and purpose in them. The more fully and frequently we participate, the more valuable traditions often become.

The season of Lent is one such tradition. For centuries, Christians have set aside the forty days before Easter as a time for reflection, repentance, and service for others. During Lent, Jesus' followers have walked step by step with their Lord to the cross, focusing intentionally on the love that led him there and on all he accomplished for us in his Easter victory.

This journal builds on that tradition. It will lead you to appropriate Bible texts, guiding you as you journal and pray about those texts. It also includes suggested service projects designed to help you demonstrate Christ's life-changing love to others.

You can use this journal alone or invite others to share the experience with you. Either way, may you grasp God's love for you more and more firmly, be led to repent more and more deeply, and grow closer and closer to the Savior who died and rose again for you!

On the lines below, consider jotting down your personal goals as you prepare your heart and reflect on our Savior's sacrifice.

Day 1 *Ash Wednesday*

> Greater love has no one than this, that someone lay down his life for his friends.
>
> *John 15:13*

Reflect

Someone once wrote a book titled *What Jesus Means to Me*. If you were to write a book like that, how would you title your chapters? (Use Jesus' own words in John 15:13 and 17:1–5 to jumpstart your thought process.)

~ from the ~
Passion Accounts

READ
John 17:1–5

Prayer Starter ~

Dear Jesus, your love is real, and it means so much more to me than I can even say. Guide me as I . . .

Day 2 *Thursday*

> God shows his love for us in that while we were still sinners, Christ died for us.
>
> Romans 5:8

Reflect

Without apology, the Bible calls us all "sinners." Our sin is not insignificant, either. Christ Jesus, God's own Son, *died* on account of it! What makes it hard to accept this reality? What makes it necessary? How does Jesus' love make it possible?

~ from the ~
Passion Accounts

READ
John 17:6–19

Prayer Starter~ **Lord, I have sinned, and it's all my fault. But my sin can't stop your very real love for me. Help me to know . . .**

Day 3 *Friday*

> In this is love, not that we have loved God but that he loved us and sent his Son.
>
> *1 John 4:10*

Reflect

You are a sinner. So am I. But Jesus came to earth to die for sinners like us! He also prays for us. He is praying for you right now. John 17:20–23 hints at what his prayers for us include. Which specific petitions mean most to you today? Why?

~ from the ~
Passion Accounts

READ
John 17:20–23

Prayer Starter~

Lord Jesus, you love me. You have always loved me. Your love is real and it is now . . .

Day 4 *Saturday*

> God, being rich in mercy, because of the great love with which he loved us, even when we were dead in our trespasses, made us alive together with Christ—by grace you have been saved—and raised us up with him and seated us with him in the heavenly places in Christ Jesus. Ephesians 2:4–6

Reflect

Read slowly through Ephesians 2:4–6 (above) and John 17:24–26. Which words or phrases strike you as most convicting today? as most encouraging? With whom could you share the encouragement?

~ from the ~

Passion Accounts

READ
John 17:24–26

Prayer Starter~ **Lord Jesus, your love is for real. It has made a way for me to be close to you now and beside you forever. Teach me to love authentically and with your very real love . . .**

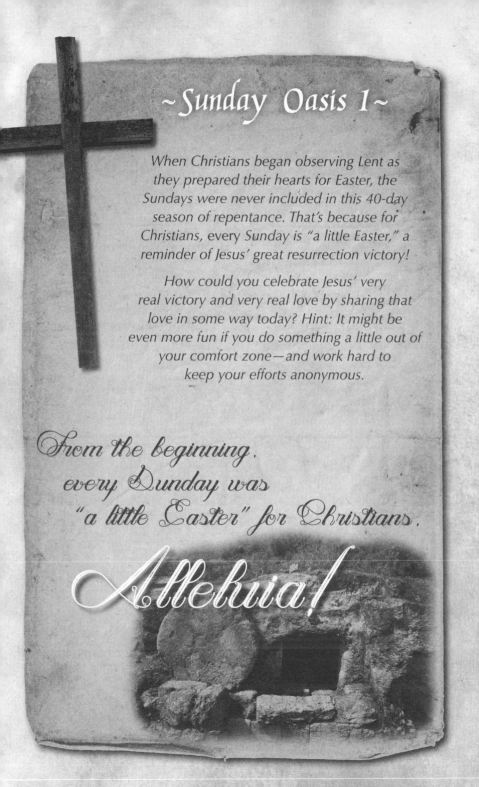

~Sunday Oasis 1~

When Christians began observing Lent as they prepared their hearts for Easter, the Sundays were never included in this 40-day season of repentance. That's because for Christians, every Sunday is "a little Easter," a reminder of Jesus' great resurrection victory!

How could you celebrate Jesus' very real victory and very real love by sharing that love in some way today? Hint: It might be even more fun if you do something a little out of your comfort zone—and work hard to keep your efforts anonymous.

From the beginning, every Sunday was "a little Easter" for Christians.

Alleluia!

Day 5 *Monday*

> As the Father has loved me,
> so have I loved you.
> Abide in my love.
>
> *John 15:9*

Reflect

How much does the Father love the Son? How much does Jesus love you? How does that love change everything? How will you "abide" in Jesus' love today?

~ from the ~
Passion Accounts

READ
Mark 11:1–10

Prayer Starter ~ Lord Jesus, just as you entered Jerusalem to shouts of praise and welcome, so enter into the events of my week with your life-changing love! . . .

Day 6 *Tuesday*

> The Father himself loves you, because you have loved me and have believed that I came from God.
>
> John 16:27

Reflect

Matthew 21:12–17 illustrates the very real difference Jesus' earthly ministry made. Some loved and believed in him. Some hated and opposed him. Still today we see these two responses. What has led you to love and believe?

~ from the ~

Passion Accounts

READ
Matthew 21:12–17

Prayer Starter ~

Lord Jesus, today I pray for those who hate and oppose you, especially . . .

Day 7 *Wednesday*

> [Jesus said,] "I made known to them your name, and I will continue to make it known, that the love with which you have loved me may be in them, and I in them."
>
> John 17:26

Reflect

The Bible includes many names for God. List as many as you can. Which is your favorite? How has Jesus "made that name known" to you? How has it energized your love for other people?

~ from the ~

Passion Accounts

READ
Matthew 21:23–32

Prayer Starter~
Lord, your enemies have always hated your name and your Word. Still, you go on loving them and working to bring them to repentance. Teach me to love and forgive as you have loved and forgiven me, especially . . .

Day 8 *Thursday*

> God's love has been poured into our hearts through the Holy Spirit who has been given to us.
>
> Romans 5:5

Reflect

In Matthew 21:42, Jesus quotes Psalm 118. He claims to be Messiah, the "cornerstone." This enrages his enemies and makes them more determined than ever to get rid of him. In what ways is Jesus the cornerstone of your life? If you remembered this more consistently, how would everything change?

~ from the ~
Passion Accounts

READ
Matthew 21:33–46

Prayer Starter ~

Dear Jesus, your faithful love is my foundation, my security, my stability. Forgive me for acting as though I am on my own . . .

Day 9 *Friday*

> Now may our Lord Jesus Christ himself, and God our Father, who loved us and gave us eternal comfort and good hope through grace, comfort your hearts and establish them in every good work and word. 2 Thessalonians 2:16–17

Reflect

In what "good works" and "good words" are you established? In other words, what habits of holiness has God worked in you as you have come to know your Savior's life-changing love? What further changes do you (and he!) want to see?

~ from the ~
Passion Accounts

READ
Matthew 22:15–33

Prayer Starter ~
Lord Jesus, repentance is a change of mind that leads to a change in heart and action. Work true repentance in me, especially as . . .

Day 10 *Saturday*

> A new commandment I give to you, that you love one another: just as I have loved you, you also are to love one another. John 13:34

Reflect

When we receive and receive and receive Christ's love, sooner or later, we overflow with it. We can't help but give it to others. In what ways would you like to be more generous with your love? Ask Jesus to work that in you.

~ from the ~

Passion Accounts

READ
Matthew 22:41–46

Prayer Starter ~

in showing love, forgive me . . .

Dear Jesus, when I'm stingy

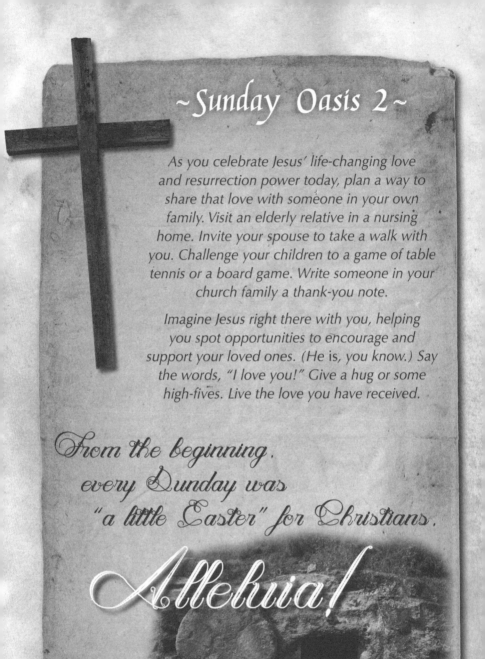

~ Sunday Oasis 2 ~

As you celebrate Jesus' life-changing love and resurrection power today, plan a way to share that love with someone in your own family. Visit an elderly relative in a nursing home. Invite your spouse to take a walk with you. Challenge your children to a game of table tennis or a board game. Write someone in your church family a thank-you note.

Imagine Jesus right there with you, helping you spot opportunities to encourage and support your loved ones. (He is, you know.) Say the words, "I love you!" Give a hug or some high-fives. Live the love you have received.

From the beginning, every Sunday was "a little Easter" for Christians.

Alleluia!

Day 11 *Monday*

Love is patient and kind.

1 Corinthians 13:4

Reflect

Many think of 1 Corinthians 13 as "the wedding chapter." And it is often read at weddings. As you study the words this week, think about how they fit both our Savior and us as we live our lives in him. How is Jesus patient and kind toward you? How are you growing in patience and kindness?

~ from the ~
Passion Accounts

READ
Mark 10:32–34

Prayer Starter~

My Savior, forgive me!
I am so often impatient and unkind. But you showed such patience with your disciples, such kindness toward your enemies! Stir up in me . . .

Day 12 *Tuesday*

> Love does not envy or boast;
> it is not arrogant or rude.
>
> *1 Corinthians 13:4–5*

Reflect

How does Luke 13:34 reflect Jesus' humility and compassion? What other examples come to mind as you think about his self-forgetful love? Forgiven in his cross, how might you become more like him in these ways?

~ from the ~
Passion Accounts

READ
Luke 13:34

Prayer Starter~ **Dear Lord, someone has described sin as being "curved in on one's self." So often, that coil of self-focus winds itself more and more tightly around my heart . . .**

Day 13 *Wednesday*

> [Love] does not insist
> on its own way.
>
> *1 Corinthians 13:5*

Reflect

In Luke 14:25–33, Jesus challenged each follower to "bear his own cross" (verse 27) and follow him. What did he mean? How does that fit in with 1 Corinthians 13:5?

~ from the ~
Passion Accounts

READ
Luke 14:25–33

Prayer Starter~

Lord Jesus, you carried my cross and died on it in my place! A thousand, thousand, thousand thanks to you, my Savior! Still, so often, instead of showing my love for you and others, I insist on getting my own way. Forgive me for . . .

Day 14 *Thursday*

> [Love] is not irritable
> or resentful.
>
> *1 Corinthians 13:5*

Reflect

Write about a time Jesus could have been irritable or resentful toward you. Then read Luke 15:1–7. How could this parable soften the hard spots of resentment and irritability in your heart?

_____

_____

_____

_____

_____

_____

_____

_____

_____

_____

~ from the ~

Passion Accounts

READ
Luke 15:1–7

_____

_____

_____

_____

_____

Prayer Starter ~

My Savior, sometimes frustrations pile up, and I just lose it! I hurt those around me, people you call me to love. Comfort me with the grace that flows from your cross. And then . . .

Day 15 *Friday*

> [Love] does not rejoice at wrongdoing, but rejoices with the truth.
>
> *1 Corinthians 13:6*

Reflect

Think about the many things that happen at your church each week. Which two or three bring you the most joy? List them. Then read Luke 19:1–10. Based on this text, what brings Jesus the most joy? How closely is your heart aligned with his?

~ from the ~
Passion Accounts

READ
Luke 19:1–10

Prayer Starter ~

Lord Jesus, draw me close to yourself, just as you drew Zacchaeus. Give me the gift of true repentance. Then align my heart ever more closely with your own heart of love, especially . . .

Day 16 *Saturday*

> Love bears all things,
> believes all things, hopes all things,
> endures all things. Love never ends.
>
> *1 Corinthians 13:7–8*

Reflect

A few days ago, we read Luke's account of Jesus weeping over unrepentant Jerusalem (Luke 13:34–35). Luke 19:41–48 gives further evidence of our Lord's grief at impenitence. Why doesn't he give up on his faithless people—including us? Think and write about that today.

~ from the ~
Passion Accounts

READ
Luke 19:41–48

Prayer Starter~

My Savior, your love never fails. You never give up on me. Your forgiveness is always there for me—the forgiveness you won on Calvary's cross. Teach me that while love is sometimes a feeling, it is always a commitment, a decision. Help me . . .

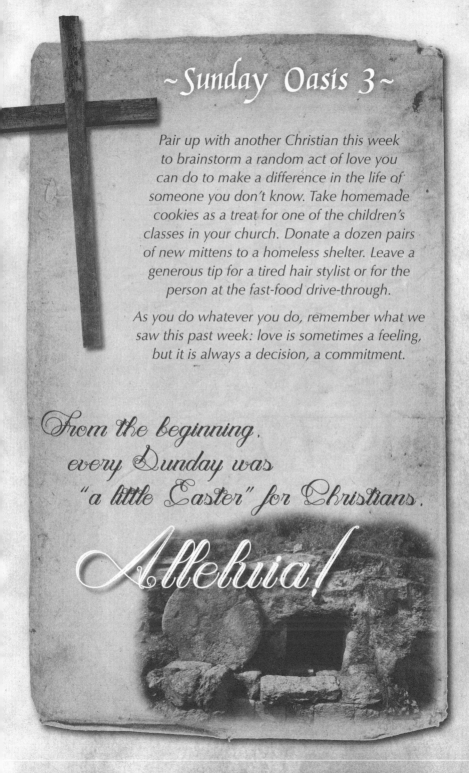

~ Sunday Oasis 3 ~

Pair up with another Christian this week to brainstorm a random act of love you can do to make a difference in the life of someone you don't know. Take homemade cookies as a treat for one of the children's classes in your church. Donate a dozen pairs of new mittens to a homeless shelter. Leave a generous tip for a tired hair stylist or for the person at the fast-food drive-through.

As you do whatever you do, remember what we saw this past week: love is sometimes a feeling, but it is always a decision, a commitment.

From the beginning, every Sunday was "a little Easter" for Christians.

Alleluia!

Day 17 *Monday*

> God is not unjust so as to overlook your work and the love that you have shown for his name in serving the saints, as you still do. Hebrews 6:10

Reflect

"Serving the saints." What better way to describe Jesus' priorities? In his cross, Christ has made us his saints, his forgiven, holy ones. Simon experienced Jesus' love. The woman who anointed Jesus experienced it. Now we have known it. How did it change their priorities? How is it changing yours?

~ from the ~
Passion Accounts

READ
Mark 14:1–11

Prayer Starter ~ **My Lord, touch me with your love in such a way that it rearranges my every priority! . . .**

Day 18 *Tuesday*

> The love of Christ controls us, because we have concluded this: that one has died for all, therefore all have died.
>
> 2 Corinthians 5:14

Reflect

Really? Does the love of Christ truly control us and our priorities? As you write today, talk with your Savior about that.

~ from the ~
Passion Accounts

READ
Mark 14:12–16

Prayer Starter ~

Dear Jesus, my priorities are often so tangled up. Yours were always clear. You saw my need. You loved me. You came to rescue me. You died. You rose again. You called me to be your own. Work this same clarity of purpose in me. Take control . . .

Day 19 *Wednesday*

> He died for all, that those who live might no longer live for themselves but for him who for their sake died and was raised. *2 Corinthians 5:15*

Reflect

Take. Eat. This is my body. This is my blood of the New Covenant. In light of 2 Corinthians 5:15, what do Jesus' words in Mark 14:22–25 mean for you? How do they change your priorities?

~ from the ~

Passion Accounts

READ
Mark 14:22–25

Prayer Starter ~
My Savior, you died for me and rose again. Forgive me for the times I live for myself. Help me . . .

Day 20 *Thursday*

> Be imitators of God, as beloved children. And walk in love, as Christ loved us and gave himself up for us, a fragrant offering and sacrifice to God. *Ephesians 5:1–2*

Reflect

Judas walked to Gethsemane to betray his Teacher. Peter walked to the High Priest's courtyard, and there denied his Lord. Jesus walked, step-by-sorrowful-step, to Calvary, determined to "give himself up for us." How did his priority change your life forever?

~ from the ~
Passion Accounts

READ
Mark 14:26–31

Prayer Starter ~

Teach me, Jesus, to walk in love, step-by-step . . .

Day 21 *Friday*

> For you were called to freedom, brothers. Only do not use your freedom as an opportunity for the flesh, but through love serve one another. *Galatians 5:13*

Reflect

In what ways are selfishness and other sinful, misplaced priorities like chains, handcuffs, and slavery? When and how were you "called to freedom"? How will you use that freedom in the days and weeks ahead?

~ from the ~
Passion Accounts

READ
Mark 14:32–42

Prayer Starter~ **Dear Savior, the disciples were free to watch and pray with you. Instead, they slept. In my life, too, other priorities often push prayer aside. Forgive my . . .**

Day 22 *Saturday*

[Jesus said,] "No one takes [my life] from me, but I lay it down of my own accord. I have authority to lay it down, and I have authority to take it up again. This charge I have received from my Father." *John 10:18*

Reflect

To an outside observer, it may have looked as though Jesus let control over his own destiny slip out of his fingers in Gethsemane. But both of today's Bible readings paint a different picture entirely. What evidence do you see that Jesus was fulfilling his top priorities? Why did he do that so willingly?

~ from the ~

Passion Accounts

READ
Matthew 26:47–56

Prayer Starter~

My Lord, given my rebellion and self-focus, it is astonishing that you would make saving me your priority! And yet, you did! . . .

~Sunday Oasis 4~

Celebrate this Sunday's "little Easter" victory by talking with your Savior in a comfortable setting. Take a walk. Sit on a hillside. Look out the window at a sunset. Kneel in a church that is open after the worshipers leave.

Look over what you have read and written in this journal so far. Talk to Jesus about the insights you have gained, the sins you want to confess, the changes his love is compelling you to make. Don't forget to thank him for the forgiveness and freedom he has won for you.

From the beginning,
every Sunday was
"a little Easter" for Christians.

Alleluia!

Day 23 *Monday*

> Grace, mercy, and peace will be with us, from God the Father and from Jesus Christ the Father's Son, in truth and love. *2 John 1:3*

Reflect

What does it mean for you that grace, mercy, and peace will be with you—be continually present for you, now and forever? What do truth and love have to do with it?

~ from the ~
Passion Accounts

READ
Matthew 26:57–68

Prayer Starter ~
Lord Jesus, you were at peace even as your enemies accused, mocked, and tortured you! Teach me how to import the peace of heaven into my heart when . . .

Day 24 *Tuesday*

> I have been crucified with Christ. It is no longer I who live, but Christ who lives in me. And the life I now live in the flesh I live by faith in the Son of God, who loved me and gave himself for me. Galatians 2:20

Reflect

Peter wept bitter tears over his denial of the Lord. If he had read Paul's words from Galatians 2:20 in later years, how would it have brought comfort to his heart? How do these words comfort you?

~ from the ~
Passion Accounts

READ
Matthew 26:69–75

Prayer Starter ~   **Lord, your death for me removes my every sin, washes away all my shame. Your life in me changes every today, bringing joy and hope. Thank you . . .**

Day 25 *Wednesday*

> Who shall separate us from the love of Christ? Shall tribulation, or distress, or persecution, or famine, or nakedness, or danger, or sword? Romans 8:35

Reflect

Not even Judas's betrayal could separate him from Jesus' love. Only Judas's rejection of Jesus' love could do that. And it did. In despair, Judas gave up on Jesus' promise of pardon and peace. When are you tempted to think today's sins are too great for God's eternal mercy? How do you know that's never true?

~ from the ~
Passion Accounts

READ
Matthew 27:1–10

Prayer Starter ~
My Savior, let the light of your unfailing love shine into every dark corner of my life today, bringing hope. Then show me how to reach out with your forgiveness to others in their darkest days . . .

Day 26 *Thursday*

> In all these things we are more
> than conquerors through
> him who loved us.
>
> Romans 8:37

Reflect

As you read Matthew 27:11–23, imagine the day Barabbas had! What must he have heard? felt? thought? In what ways are *you* Barabbas? How does thinking about this change today and every day?

~ from the ~
Passion Accounts

READ
Matthew 27:11–23

Prayer Starter~
Dear Jesus, if not for you, my predicament would be far worse even than that of Barabbas, imprisoned in his deepest dungeon. But because of you and your love, I am more than a conqueror! . . .

Day 27 *Friday*

> Since we belong to the day, let us be sober, having put on the breastplate of faith and love, and for a helmet the hope of salvation. For God has not destined us for wrath, but to obtain salvation through our Lord Jesus Christ.
>
> 1 Thessalonians 5:8–9

Reflect

Because Pontius Pilate "delivered [Jesus] to be crucified" (Matthew 27:26), you have an entirely new destiny! Because Jesus was stripped and scourged, you can put on the "breastplate of faith and love." You can wear the "hope of salvation" as a helmet. How does this work in you a bold and holy hope today?

~ from the ~

Passion Accounts

READ
Matthew 27:24–26

Prayer Starter ~ My Savior, forgive my timidity and fear. Grant me the courage I need today to . . .

Day 28 *Saturday*

> May the Lord make you increase and abound in love for one another and for all, as we do for you, so that he may establish your hearts blameless in holiness before our God and Father, at the coming of our Lord Jesus with all his saints. *1 Thessalonians 3:12–13*

Reflect

In the end, Jesus lost everything—his dignity, his clothes, his friends, his rights, and, ultimately, his life. But his enemies did not take these from him. He willingly gave them up to gain an eternity with you! How does this change the way you think about yourself? How does it cultivate generosity in your heart?

~ from the ~
Passion Accounts

READ
Matthew 27:27–30

Prayer Starter ~

Dear Jesus, yesterday is gone. Tomorrow may not find me here on earth. Show me how to use today in generous response to your self-giving love . . .

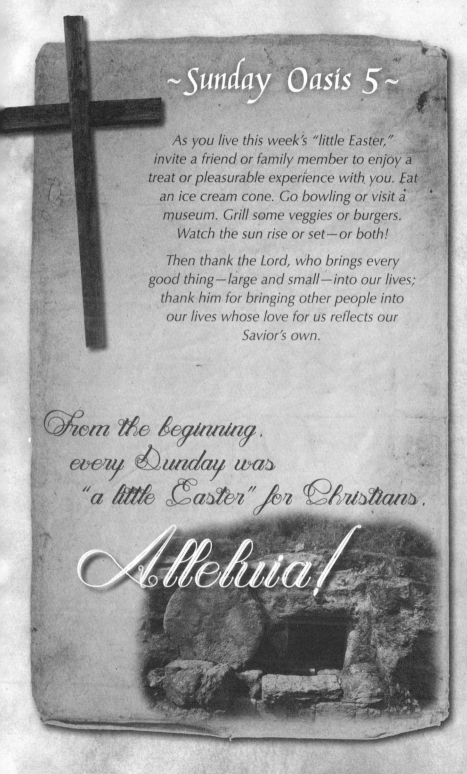

~Sunday Oasis 5~

As you live this week's "little Easter," invite a friend or family member to enjoy a treat or pleasurable experience with you. Eat an ice cream cone. Go bowling or visit a museum. Grill some veggies or burgers. Watch the sun rise or set—or both!

Then thank the Lord, who brings every good thing—large and small—into our lives; thank him for bringing other people into our lives whose love for us reflects our Savior's own.

From the beginning,
every Sunday was
"a little Easter" for Christians.

Alleluia!

Day 29 *Monday*

> "What no eye has seen, nor ear heard, nor the heart of man imagined, what God has prepared for those who love him"—these things God has revealed to us through the Spirit. For the Spirit searches everything, even the depths of God.
>
> *1 Corinthians 2:9–10*

Reflect

As you have written in this journal over the past days and weeks, what truths new and old has God revealed to you through the Spirit? How do these truths change today and every tomorrow?

~ from the ~

Passion Accounts

READ
John 19:16–22

Prayer Starter ~
Dear Jesus, you are King and Lord of all. So often, I think of sin as trivial. I take my own guilt lightly, overlooking and excusing it. Forgive . . .

Day 30 *Tuesday*

The grace of the Lord Jesus Christ and the love of God and the fellowship of the Holy Spirit be with you all. *2 Corinthians 13:14*

Reflect

Peace. Violence. Love. Loathing. As you write now, contrast the benediction of 2 Corinthians 13:14 with the death by which Jesus won this blessing for us (Matthew 27:32–44; John 19:23–24). Also contrast the future that would have been yours with the future that awaits you because of Jesus.

~ from the ~

Passion Accounts

READ
Matthew 27:32–44;
John 19:23–24

Prayer Starter~ **My Savior, forgive me for taking your love for granted, for assuming that I deserve the peace you won for me. . . .**

Day 31 *Wednesday*

> It is my prayer that your love may abound more and more, with knowledge and all discernment, so that you may approve what is excellent, and so be pure and blameless for the day of Christ. *Philippians 1:9-10*

Reflect

On Calvary's cross, Jesus hung "enthroned," as it were: the King of love, granting pardon even to those who were mocking and murdering him. Throughout all eternity, Jesus will reign in glory, King and Lord of all. Where do you see yourself in these two snapshots?

~ from the ~
Passion Accounts

READ
Luke 23:32–38

Prayer Starter ~ King Jesus, teach me to live today as a forgiven, immortal heir of heaven . . .

Day 32 *Thursday*

> Then I looked, and I heard around the throne and the living creatures and the elders the voice of many angels, numbering myriads of myriads and thousands of thousands, saying with a loud voice, "Worthy is the Lamb who was slain, to receive power and wealth and wisdom and might and honor and glory and blessing!" Revelation 5:11–12

Reflect

Just as John took Mary into his own home and cared for her, so Jesus will one day invite us into the Father's house to care for us! What will that be like?

~ from the ~
Passion Accounts

READ
John 19:25–27

Prayer Starter ~
Jesus, you are my Savior, my King, and my Brother. Because you came to live and die for me on earth, I will one day live with you in the New Creation! As I live out that destiny today . . .

Day 33 *Friday*

> In fact Christ has been raised from the dead, the firstfruits of those who have fallen asleep. For as by a man came death, by a man has come also the resurrection of the dead.
>
> *1 Corinthians 15:20–21*

Reflect

Christ has died. Christ is risen. Christ will come again. These ten simple words express the foundational truths of the Christian faith. As you journal today, write about each of these three sentences.

~ from the ~
Passion Accounts

READ
John 19:28–37

Prayer Starter ~ Dear Lord, your death has brought me life! . . .

Day 34 *Saturday*

> *Death is swallowed up in victory.*
>
> 1 Corinthians 15:54

Reflect

Before you think and write about today's Scripture verses, consider first taking a walk through a cemetery. If that isn't possible, find a photo of a cemetery online and read today's Scriptures with that photo as a backdrop. What details from the texts become more poignant or powerful in light of your walk or the photo you found?

~ from the ~
Passion Accounts

READ
John 19:38-42

Prayer Starter ~

My Savior, your death changes everything about my future. . . .

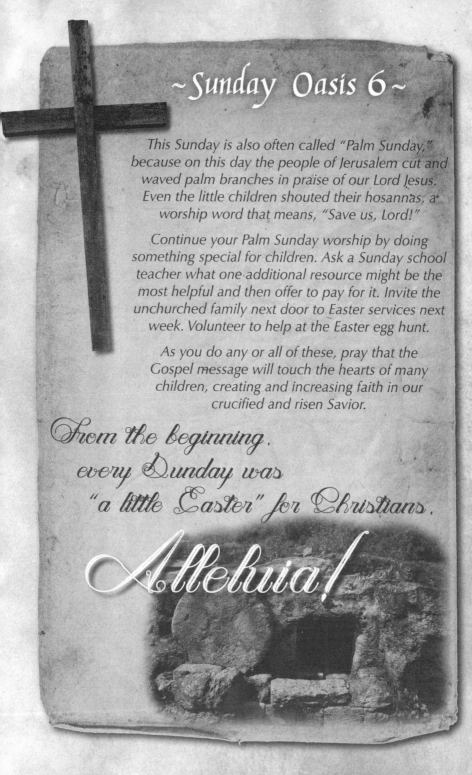

~ Sunday Oasis 6 ~

This Sunday is also often called "Palm Sunday," because on this day the people of Jerusalem cut and waved palm branches in praise of our Lord Jesus. Even the little children shouted their hosannas, a worship word that means, "Save us, Lord!"

Continue your Palm Sunday worship by doing something special for children. Ask a Sunday school teacher what one additional resource might be the most helpful and then offer to pay for it. Invite the unchurched family next door to Easter services next week. Volunteer to help at the Easter egg hunt.

As you do any or all of these, pray that the Gospel message will touch the hearts of many children, creating and increasing faith in our crucified and risen Savior.

From the beginning, every Sunday was "a little Easter" for Christians.

Alleluia!

Day 35 *Monday*

> The crowds that went before him and that followed him were shouting, "Hosanna to the Son of David! Blessed is he who comes in the name of the Lord! Hosanna in the highest!" *Matthew 21:9*

Reflect

Stand in Jerusalem with the Palm Sunday crowd. Pretend not to know what will happen by the week's end. What would you have seen, heard, smelled, felt? Write about it. Now, repeat the experience with the cross and empty tomb clearly in mind. What changes?

~ from the ~
Passion Accounts

READ
Matthew 21:1–11

Prayer Starter ~ Hosanna! Save, Lord!
Please use this Holy Week to continue the healing, transforming work you have begun in my heart and life. . . .

Day 36 *Tuesday*

[Jesus said,] "The hour has come for the Son of Man to be glorified. Truly, truly, I say to you, unless a grain of wheat falls into the earth and dies, it remains alone; but if it dies, it bears much fruit." John 12:23–24

Reflect

As you reflect on today's Scripture readings, zero in on what Jesus says his death will accomplish. How is the mission he accomplished life-giving and life-changing for you personally?

~ from the ~

Passion Accounts

READ
John 12:27–36

Prayer Starter~ **My Savior, you knew exactly what was about to happen to you, but you walked courageously forward, into the very jaws of hell—for me! . . .**

Day 37 *Wednesday*

> [Jesus] said to his disciples, "You know that after two days the Passover is coming, and the Son of Man will be delivered up to be crucified."
>
> Matthew 26:1–2

Reflect

How did the unnamed woman in Matthew 26 honor Jesus? How did he honor her? How has he honored you? How are you honoring him?

~ from the ~
Passion Accounts

READ
Matthew 26:1–13

Prayer Starter ~
Your love, Lord, is life-giving and life-changing. The woman in Matthew 26 clearly shows this! I want my life to show it clearly, too. So please . . .

Day 38 *Holy Thursday*

> [Jesus said,] "You call me Teacher and Lord, and you are right, for so I am. If I then, your Lord and Teacher, have washed your feet, you also ought to wash one another's feet." John 13:13–14

Reflect

Last actions. Final words. These usually carry special significance. We choose them with extra care. We remember them in vivid detail. Write about Jesus' last actions and final words to his disciples as you reflect on today's Bible readings.

~ from the ~
Passion Accounts

READ
*Matthew 26:26–30;
John 13:1–20.*

Prayer Starter~
Dear Jesus, your love has given me life. Knowing you has changed my life. As I continue to reflect on that love in the days ahead, please . . .

Day 39 *Good Friday*

> Jesus cried out again with a loud voice and yielded up his spirit.
>
> Matthew 27:50

Reflect

What ended at the cross? What began there? Make two lists, each as long as possible. What difference do these endings and beginnings make?

~ from the ~

Passion Accounts

READ
John 13:31–35

Prayer Starter~ *My Savior, if your love were an ocean, it would be bottomless. If it were the sky, it would soar up and up forever . . .*

Day 40 *Holy Saturday*

> The sting of death is sin, and the power of sin is the law. But thanks be to God, who gives us the victory through our Lord Jesus Christ.
>
> 1 Corinthians 15:56–57

Reflect

Divide the passage above into five segments and jot down your thoughts related to each of them. How do these words add to your understanding that Jesus' death and resurrection are life-giving and life-changing?

~ from the ~
Passion Accounts

READ
Matthew 27:62–66

Prayer Starter ~

Lord Jesus, you have given me the victory, an eternal victory! As I celebrate your resurrection . . .

He has risen, as he said.
Matthew 28:6

Alleluia!
Christ is risen!

Reflect

How have you changed over the past several weeks as you have meditated on the Scriptures, prayed, and served others? In light of Christ's love at work in you, what do you understand more fully? What do you believe more deeply? To what have you committed more whole-heartedly?

~ from the ~
Resurrection Accounts

READ
Matthew 28:1–20

Prayer Starter~
Lord Jesus, your love changes everything! . . .

This Love Changes Everything

This is love, not that
we have loved God
but that he loved us.

1 John 4:10

Now after the Sabbath, toward the dawn of the first day of the week, Mary Magdalene and the other Mary went to see the tomb. And behold, there was a great earthquake, for an angel of the Lord descended from heaven and came and rolled back the stone and sat on it. His appearance was like lightning, and his clothing white as snow. And for fear of him the guards trembled and became like dead men.

But the angel said to the women, "Do not be afraid, for I know that you seek Jesus who

was crucified. He is not here, for he has risen, as he said. Come, see the place where he lay. Then go quickly and tell his disciples that he

has risen from the dead,

and behold, he is going before you to Galilee; there you will see him. See, I have told you."

So they departed quickly from the tomb with fear and great joy, and ran to tell his disciples.

Matthew 28:1–8

"Death is
swallowed up in victory."
"O death,
where is your victory?
O death,
where is your sting?"

The sting of death is sin, and
the power of sin is the law. But
thanks be to God, who gives us
the victory through our Lord
Jesus Christ.

1 Corinthians 15:54–57

If in Christ we have hope in this life only,
we are of all people most to be pitied.

But in fact Christ has been raised from the dead,
the firstfruits of those who have fallen asleep. For
as by a man came death, by a man has come
also the resurrection of the dead.

1 Corinthians 15:19–21

For this reason, because I have heard of your faith in the Lord Jesus and your love toward all the saints, I do not cease to give thanks for you, remembering you in my prayers, that the God of our Lord Jesus Christ, the Father of glory, may give you the Spirit of wisdom and of revelation in the knowledge of him, having the eyes of your hearts enlightened, that you may know what is the hope to which he has called you, what are the riches of his glorious inheritance in the saints, and what is the immeasurable greatness of his power toward us who believe. Ephesians 1:15–19

Alleluia! Christ is risen!

To see all of CTA's books, visit us at www.CTAinc.com.

If this book has made a difference in
your life or if you have simply enjoyed it,
we would like to hear from you.
Your words will encourage us! If you
have suggestions for us to consider as
we create books like this in the future,
please send those, too.

We invite you to post your comments at
http://share.ctainc.com/

Or you can reach us by e-mail at editor@CTAinc.
com. Please include the subject line: LCE5PJ

You can also contact us at:

Editorial Coordinator
Department LCE5PJ
CTA, Inc.
PO Box 1205
Fenton, MO 63026-1205